Waking

Waking

RON RASH

HUB CITY PRESS
SPARTANBURG, SC

First printing, October 2011

Book design: Emily Louise Smith
Printed in Saline, MI
by McNaughton & Gunn, Inc.
Cover photograph © Tom Fowlks/Getty

TEXT Janson Pro 9.8/13.5
DISPLAY Futura 11

Library of Congress
Cataloging-in-Publication Data

Rash, Ron, 1953–
  Waking / Ron Rash.
p. cm.
ISBN 978-1-891885-82-2 (alk. paper)
  1. North Carolina—Poetry.
  2. Mountain life—Poetry.
  3. Southern States—Poetry.
  I. Title.
PS3568.A698W35 2011
811'.54—dc22
2011008143

186 W. Main Street
Spartanburg, SC 29306
www.hubcity.org

FOR *Joyce Brown and Earl Holder*

CONTENTS

v.

Resolution

The surge and clatter of whitewater conceals
how shallow underneath is, how quickly gone.
Leave that noise behind. Come here
where the water is slow, and clear.
Watch the crawfish prance across the sand,
the mica flash, the sculpen blend with stone.
It's all beyond your reach though it appears
as near and known as your outstretched hand.

I

First Memory

Dragonflies dip, rise. Their backs
catch light, purple like church glass.
Gray barn planks balance on stilts,
walk toward the pond's deep end.
A green smell simmers shallows,
where tadpoles flow like black tears.
Minnows lengthen their shadows.
Something unseen stirs the reeds.

The Trout in the Springhouse

Caught by my uncle
in the Watauga River,
brought back in a bucket
because some believed
its gills were like filters,
that pureness poured into
the springhouse's trough pool,
and soon it was thriving
on sweet corn and biscuits,
guarding that spring-gush,
brushing my fingers
as I swirled the water
up in my palm cup
tasted its quickness
swimming inside me.

Milking Traces

The paths between pasture, barn
were no straight lines but slow curves
around a hill that centered
thirty acres. To a child
those narrow levels seemed like
belts worn on the hill's bulged waist,
if climbed straight up, tall steps for
stone Aztec ruins—though razed
each time dawnlight peaked landrise,
belts and steps became sudden
contrails from planets circling
the sun's blaze, planets disguised
with cow hide, the furrowed skin
of an old woman's visage.

Sleepwalking

Strange how I never once woke
in a hall, on a porch step,
but always outside, bare feet
slick with dew-grass, the house
deeper shadow, while above
moon leaning its round shoulder
to the white oak's limbs, stars thrown
skyward like fistfuls of jacks.
Rising as if from water
the way dark lightened, it all
slow-returning, reluctant,
as though while I'd been sleeping
summoned away to attend
matters other than a child's
need for a world to be in.

Woodshed in Watauga County

Leaking in the one window,
candle shallow, then deepened,
caught-light gathered on gray planks
like a bowl filling slowly,
a simmer of late summer
distilled to dull yellow glow,
thickening air like honey
as mud daubers and dust motes
drifted above like moments
unmoored from time, and the world
and the sun aligned, grew still.

Junk Car in Snow

No shade tree surgery could
revive its engine, so rolled
into the pasture, left stalled
among cattle, soon rust-scabs
breaking out on blue paint, tires
sagging like leaky balloons,
yet when snow came, magical,
an Appalachian igloo
I huddled inside, cracked glass
my window as I watched snow
smooth pasture as though a quilt
for winter to rest upon,
and how quiet it was—the creek
muffled by ice, gray squirrels
curled in leaf beds, the crows mute
among stark lifts of branches,
only the sound of my own
white breath dimming the window.

Time Flow

Green plush of bank moss, a smell
like after rain, and the creek
deepening behind the shed
where Nolan White spent his time
to wedge hours and seconds
out of time, free them to spill
out the open door as if
another current flowing
through the pool where I sank worms
to raise watery rainbows.
His one son had died, so now
he worked alone, making clocks
for Boone tourists. Once I laid
down my tackle, stepped inside
a moth-swirl of ticks and chimes,
at the center lathed chestnut
laid upon two sawhorses,
what Nolan White bent over,
hands dipping in, attentive
as a surgeon as he set
each gear in place. When it stirred
he brought me close, let me hear
that one pulse among many.

The Wallet

Knee deep in the Watauga's
rock leaping whitewater,
my brother loses his balance,
his life if our father
doesn't flail downstream
swimming air, running river,
tripping on stones to collar
his son, drag to a sandbar,
confirm with tentative fingers
his empty back pocket.
We pace back and forth on the shoreline,
down to the bridge, the other bank
before the sun finally falls
blurring the river in darkness,
my father not saying, *don't worry*,
a life is priceless, not saying
something like that, not tousling
my brother's hair and smiling.
For this is October. My father
believes he'll be fired soon,
will face winter's cold coming
without thirty-four washed-away dollars.

Myopia

They belonged to the mother
of my grandmother, removed
the morning she died, each lens
a clear coin, arms and rims
tarnished gold wire, folded in
their black velvet-lined casket
two decades, until I wiped
dust from each lens, let my face
look out a window to see
the world as she did, and saw
a gray blur become a barn,
apples emerge from green sleeves
of branches, and told no one.

Charley Starnes

After the woods a sudden
swoon of light in a clearing
and I am where I was then,
that summer morning I brought
food to Charley Starnes who drank
rotgut whiskey so he might
douse the memory of gas
searing his lungs, the bullet
that almost opened his heart.
Say sir, my grandmother said,
gave me the tin of biscuits,
mason jar of soup before
I walked the fence line and through
the woodshed's board-gaps watched him
sway back and forth before flames
that seemed fueled by his curses,
and what burned inside the drum
I never knew, but left all
I'd brought on the porch, then fled
the place where six months later
sleeve or shirttail dipped too close
and Charley Starnes wore a suit
of flames through barbed wire, into
a corn field where they found him
face down like a felled scarecrow,
shattered stalks marking his swerve
and lunge through rows as though
a man trying to dodge fire.

Watauga County: 1959

On Clay Ridge a crescent moon
balanced itself, soon became
an open parenthesis
no father, uncle could close
as we hunched on farmhouse steps,
wore Sunday clothes days early,
what conversation the rasp
of matches. Small blades of flame
rose to faces no tears marked
as I heard silence widen
like fish swirls on a calm pond,
touch the last fence he had strung,
the tractor in the far field
already starting to rust.

II

Bonding Fire

For Bob Cumming

A spark takes hold in a glen
in Scotland's midlands and burns
winter and summer, and when
hands tending that spark grow cold

passed on to daughter and son
fire passed hearth to hearth to fire
a bride's wedding night passion,
light an old man's corpse candle,

part heirloom, part talisman,
cradled and nursed like a child
in the ship's hold when the clan
sailed west to Charleston, then west

to east Tennessee, the fire
carried by wagon, by hand,
huddled by when a panther
cried out at night or when night

turned slantland white when they came
into the Blue Ridge where they
raised their hearths over a flame
two centuries old, two more

passing until water came
to douse that valley, to douse
the hearth of one who remained
to tend that fire, who refused

to leave the valley until
that fire left with him, the truck's
windows left up less wind still
the pail of sparks his lap held.

Pocketknives

Carried like time, consulted
as often when the sermon
droned on past noon, hay bailer
broke a chain, any other
lingering moments their scarred
and calloused workflesh idled,
the blades pried free the way wives
might slip a ribbon, that same
delicate tug when forge-craft
sharpened what light sun or bulb
provided as they trimmed dirt
from the undersides of nails,
surfaced splinters, bled blisters,
a tool made more than a tool
each time they rasped a whetstone
across steel until it flashed
pure as silver, then a rag
doused in oil to rub new-bright
the handles hewed from antler,
pearl, stained wood grain, ivory
laced with brass or gold, the one
vanity of men caught once
when dead in a coat and tie,
so ordered from catalogs,
saved and traded for, searched for
in sheds and fields if lost, passed
father to son as heirlooms,
like talismans carried close
to the bone, cloaked as the hearts
of these men who rarely spoke
their fears and hopes, let their words
clench inside a locked silence.

Shadetree

After Sunday noon-dinner
men gathered where truck or car
motor hung from an oak limb
like some trophy shot or yanked
from wood or river, and though
all had their views on just how
and what needed to be done,
not one took off his cufflinks,
rolled his sleeves around biceps.
Cigarette butts and Red Man
marked an afternoon's passing
as each held his place as if
before a hearth, the log-chained
weld of steel hanging sometimes
for a month, huddled around
so it might spark and fuel
an allowance of language
beyond utility, though
always first the lexicon
of engines before slow shift
to story, joke and sometimes
the hotwired valves and pistons
making racket in the heart.

Car Tags

I have seen them as spare parts
on combines and hay balers,
poor man's wind chimes, a scarecrow's
loud jewelry, though my uncle
nailed his to the barn as if
patchwork armor, and after
five decades those rows of tin
lined up like a calendar
of one man's life weathering
sun and rain, mountain winters,
years rubbing away as rust
made the past harder to read
on heartwood warped and buckling
under the burden of time.

Muskellunge

It came with spring's high water,
seen first by boys on the bridge,
their wide-apart palms dismissed
until part of that pool slammed
Mike Hartley's Panther Martin
so hard his rod snapped and he
claimed no brown or rainbow had
broken his rod. After that
false dawn to last light always
at least one man offering
nightcrawler, minnow, wood plug,
spoon, spinner, mouse, anything
that might bring to surface what
the county's game warden called
a muskellunge, giving name
to that long, sleek flesh prowling
shallows like a torpedo.
Then late summer came, the pool
a thin clear like a mirror,
the big fish harboring deep
beneath cutbanks, coming out
only at last light, watched for
by men on the bridge who now
rarely made casts. It vanished
at the end of September
when four-day's rain flushed away
the wood-weir beaver had built
to slow the tailrace's flow—
though some believed it still there,
and for years would pause each time
they crossed that bridge, eyes searching
the pool for swirl or fin-surge,
a shadow lurking beneath,
gaining depth, becoming real.

Tobacco Barn

A scary place for a child alone:
tobacco hanging from rafters like bats,
leaves dim as dust, as old windows,
same color as the copperhead
Uncle Howard killed near the spring.

Older eyes saw green changed to gold,
leaves crisp as new dollar bills,
a promise close as a raised hand,
chastened each time dark clouds rumbled
across Grandfather Mountain toward Dismal,
too late in the year to be welcomed.

Spillcorn

The road is now a shadow
of a road, overgrown with
scrub pine, blackjack oak. Years back
one of my kinsmen logged here,
a man needing steady work
no hailstorm or August drought
could take away, so followed
Spillcorn Creek into the gorge,
brought with him a mule and sled,
a Colt revolver to kill
the rattlesnakes, and always
tucked in his lunch sack a book:
history, sometimes novel
from the Marshall library,
so come midday he might rest
his spine against bark and read—
what had roughed his hands now smooth
as his fingertips turned
the leaves, each word whispered soft
as the wind reading the trees.

Emrys

Lamp and candle, a lantern
fetched from the barn not enough,
more light needed to fling back
shadow-quilts on the birth-bed,
labor a breach child to life,
so the husband sent horseback
from Dismal Gorge, riding north
toward Blowing Rock, Joe Black's farm,
the one car close by, and soon
that Model T bumping down
logging roads thinned to cow paths,
light hauled deep into Dismal
like two long lengths of lumber—
and finally there, the cabin's
one door propped, light flooding in
as the midwife probes and cuts,
men turn their heads while women
heat water, bring out clean cloths,
and just before dawn a child
brought forth blinking and squalling,
the great-aunt speaking one word
carried deep in blood-memory,
crossing time and an ocean
to name this child born of light.

Mirror

Ordered from Winston-Salem,
hauled by train far as Lenoir,
unboxed, bundled in blankets,
wagoned north to Blowing Rock,
jolted across Middlefork,
geed and hawed uphill while hands
braced it from sliding where land
slanted sharp as a barn roof,
before finally there, and then
brought through doors like a body,
unwrapped and uprighted so
after five years of breaking
land that had tried to break her,
after three children, so long
seeing her face only in
wrinkles of water, she'll stand
free of her bedclothes, alone
inside the mirror's embrace,
let face, breasts, child-widened hips,
come clear in first light and find
only herself, which is all
she wishes for this moment.

Rebecca Boone

It could not be unraveled
what she had sown that winter
he wandered the Blue Ridge where
women with hair black as hers
knew her husband's tongue only
when lips pressed deep, shared one breath.
She could not know if he found
some part of her absence from
another's night-touch, freed by
darkness to see what was wished,
as she had when she believed
him months dead—those evenings his
brother's face dimmed familiar,
corn shucks rasped and shuddered while
hearth-gloam wove quilts of shadow
across cabin walls, the bed
where need and memory merged.
A Boone anyhow, he said,
that fall they reunited,
then lifted the newborn, smiled
at a face more his own than
even he could understand.

Woman Among Lightning: Catawba County Fair, 1962

Tendrils of neon sprouting
sudden as kudzu across
seven acres of sawdust,
in the middle a great wheel
dredging buckets of darkness
out of the sky, and this night
wind flapping tents, underneath
of clouds glowing like blown coals,
thundering their heavy freight
toward the fairground as riders
disembark early, but she
refuses, so rides into
the storm, hand reaching as if
trying to pull lightning-wreaths
around her head—a farmwife
leaving the ground where her days
are measured in rows, the hoe
swinging like a metronome
while life leaks away like blood
on land always wanting more,
wanting more, free of it now
as the hawk she saw at dawn,
wings embracing an updraft,
how it hovered that moment
above the fields and fence wire,
as she does now at the pause
between ascent and return,
far from earth as a fistful
of hard-earned quarters can take her.

III

Bloodroot

Two weeks without frost will bloom
trout lily and bloodroot while
sun soaking through gorge-rocks stirs
the gorgon heads underneath,
unknotting, rising through veins
in granite, split tongues tasting
bright air, divining heat-spill
where outcrops pool the noon sun
and I come with my snake stick,
work my way upridge. They pay
by the foot, those handlers who
lift these snakes on Sunday nights,
holy fools, I call them though
I was too, before four years
away at Bible College,
schooling they helped pay for so
I could better learn the Word,
learned instead the world, returned
a felled angel, my God now
a bottle of Jack Daniels
held like prayer, my service
work I find when someone needs
barbed wire strung up, sheet rock hung,
whatever else gets the bills
in Randy Davidson's hand,
liquor rising behind him
like Jacob's Ladder, the ring
of his register sweeter
than a preacher's altar call.
Serpents pay best, satinbacks
old folks call them, big ones sell
for thirty dollars, so springs
I climb this ridge, always hear
the hum of resurrection

as I near, the pillowcase
filling with a muscled flow
like water in a suckhole,
and when I've caught all I can,
take them to Reverend Holten,
who does not know I listen
beneath the window those nights
he and the congregation kneel
on concrete, pray for my lost
backslid soul in vain before
they raise their serpents and I
raise mine that it might crawl down
my throat, settle and coil,
still the rattling in my heart.

The Reaping

As supper cools, fireflies spark
dew-grass like stars on a pond
and still the hay baler hums
in the meadow, he does not
need an owl cry or his wife's
linger by window to know
what keeps his son in the field's
gathering darkness, so steps
through barbed wire strung in April,
already sagged by fence posts
leaned like corn stalks after hail
because the boy would not
listen, would always search for
short cuts, even as a child
leaving weeds between bean rows,
cheating on nails when a shed
needed shingles, each short cut
leading to this evening when
his father smells blood sizzling
on the metal and as he
frees an arm from the roller
chides his son for half a life
lost to save half a minute,
before kissing the cold brow,
forgives what the reaper cannot.

Dismal

No passing traveler named this place,
could utter sudden-tongued such bleak
syllables. No, this word rose
from years of breaking hoes and backs
against a leached-out, angled ground,
that grudgingly gave up each rock,
yet freed like Bible plagues the nests
of yellow jackets, rattlesnakes,
though fog was worst, how it settled
for days to snuff out light and sound,
rot barbed wire, fence posts and grain.
No gaze but inward in a world
gray and still as any gravestone.

Hearth

Two days and a night snow fell,
cold closing on Spillcorn Cove
tight as a bear trap, and held
kin close to their fires until

the eighth day when sun began
to raise their world out of white,
and on the far ridge a smudge
of smoke above the tree line,

proof the old man had weathered
another hard winter though
a nephew went to make sure,
and found the porch, back room gone,

by the hearth one man, what he
decades back raised to surround
granite slab, corbelled chimney
mainly smoke and hearth-ash now,

crowbarred oak plank by oak plank,
fed to the fire, a cabin
unbuilding itself back to
the stone core when it began.

Tobacco

Before the dream of tobacco, golden
as it cured inside our October barns,
we thought our land generous enough,
apple trees drooping their fruit to our hands,
woods and streams thick with squirrels and trout.
We planted our oats and corn and wheat and beans.
Some crops were lost but the springhouse filled,
always enough to get us through the winter.

But then the fence laws passed and taxes rose.
We needed cash crops to keep our farms.
We heard the legends of men who had less
land than us but now were men of ease,
who lived in columned houses tobacco raised,
knew if they were rich then we were poor,
so tobacco came and our world changed.

We bought those bitter seeds, the fertilizer,
the poison for the worms. In January
we set out plant beds and later broke
the best ground in our bottomlands.
Then came the kind of toil we'd never known,
plowing, chopping, suckering, and topping.
We left beans and corn unhoed, let weeds
strangle our fields, the apple trees
unpruned in the orchard as we spent
days kneeling to tobacco, our blistered hands
each leaf a small, green flame
even a summer breeze might snuff.

By fall some blight or drought or sudden rain
had wiped out all our crop or most of it.
When a good year came that only meant
other farmers did as well. We'd watch

prices drop ten cents a pound.
Good harvest or bad we sank deeper in debt,
and planted more tobacco to get out,
and every year our dream slipped away like smoke,
which was all it was, all it would ever be.

Elegy for Merle Watson

Nothing's on the level in this terrain.
A tractor can lose its balance quick as a heart.
One tractor wheel turns in the morning light.
One hand clutches the earth, trying to hold on.
"Wayfaring Stranger," "Deep River Blues,"
those fatalistic mountain hymns became you.

Tonight your father cradles his guitar.
A stage half-empty confirms what we don't hear,
what does not echo, fill the runs and lines.
Musician, distant kin, your silence survives.

Blue Cat

Like a pirate's hook, that gaff
the old man roped to his wrist
each spring to probe where logfall
and slow flow calmed the river,
places where arm-long blue cats
gathered to spawn, though he swore
one was longer, its whiskers
waving like whips, black eyes big
as marbles, just a tall tale
until his body washed up
on a sandbar, his gaff still
set deep in the great finned back.

White Wings

Tucked in each pew's back pocket,
hymnals simmered in mote dust
until Sundays when the soiled
rough hands of farmers lifted
those songbibles, pages spread
like white wings being set free,
but what rose was one voice
woven from many, and heard
by Jason Storey who stood
in a field half an acre
of gravestones away, mute as
a fence post while neighbors sang
inside the church doors he swore
never to pass through after
wife and son died in childbirth,
that long ago Christmas when
three days of snow made the road
to Blowing Rock disappear,
the doctor brought on horseback
arriving too late. Decades
Jason Storey would remain
true to his word, yet was there
in that field come rain or cold,
but came no closer, between
church and field two marble stones,
angel-winged, impassible.

The Girl in the River

Men tried three days to raise her
with prayers, grabbling hooks trolled
like lures across the suckhole,
the divers finally called in
to work water's other side,
where they swirled above a face
clear as a lover's, but could
not reach her though one came close
enough to brush the yellow
flow of hair and almost drown
before others roped him back.
After that they watched from shore,
let drought leech the river's strength,
waked damp and gasping from dreams
of her cold, beckoning eyes.

Resonance

No rain for weeks, White Ash Creek
a dried scab, lake miles away,
nothing but flame, smoke, and heat,
kept at bay by men blackfaced

as miners after a shift,
including those who will see
myth-dreams awakened, a trout
alive in a burning tree,

branch-caught by the gill, closing
and opening its mouth as though
the smoke a murky upstream
it has to make its way through

to reach the hundred gallon
sky pool it spilled from, and when
flames flagshift, the trout is gone
back into The Mabinogion.

Three A.M. and the Stars Were Out

When the phone rings way too late
for good news, just another
farmer wanting me to lose
half a night's sleep and drive some
backcountry wash-out for miles,
fix what he's botched, on such nights
I'm like an old, drowsy god
tired of answering prayers,
so let it ring a while, hope
they might hang up, though of course
they don't, don't because they know
the younger vets shuck off these
dark expeditions to me,
thinking it's my job, not theirs,
because I've done it so long
I'm used to such nights, because
old as I am I'll still do
what they refuse to, and soon
I'm driving out of Marshall
headed north, most often toward
Shelton Laurel, toward some barn
where a calf that's been bad-bred
to save stud fees is trying
to be born, or a cow laid
out in a barn stall, dying
of milk fever, easily cured
if a man hadn't wagered
against his own dismal luck,
waited too late, hoping to
save my fee for a salt lick,
roll of barbed wire, and it's not
all his own fault, poor too long
turns the smartest man stupid,
makes him see nothing beyond

a short term gain, which is why
I know more likely than not
I'll be arriving too late,
what's to be done best done with
rifle or shotgun, so make
driving the good part, turn off
my radio, let the dark
close around until I know
a kind of loneliness that
doesn't feel sad as I pass
the homes of folks I don't know,
may never know, but wonder
what they are dreaming, what life
they wake to—thinking such things,
or sometimes just watching for
what stays unseen except on
country roads after midnight,
the copperheads soaking up
what heat the blacktop still holds,
foxes and bobcats, one time
in the fifties a panther,
yellow eyes bright as truck beams,
black-tipped tail swishing before
leaping away through the trees,
back into its extinction,
all this thinking and watching
keeping my mind off what waits
on up the road, worst of all
the calves I have to pull one
piece at a time, birthing death.
Though sometimes it all works out.
I turn a calf's head and then
like a safe's combination
the womb unlocks, calf slides free,

or this night when stubborn life
got back on its feet, round eyes
clear and hungry, my I.V.
stuck in its neck, and I take
my time packing up, ask for
a second cup of coffee,
so I can linger awhile
in the barn mouth watching stars
awake in their wide pasture.

IV

Genealogy

From Wales to Murderkill Hundred, then
in one generation down the Shenandoah,
to North Carolina where tombstones raised
a topography of accident and will
across three mountain counties, otherwise
crossing only centuries. Perhaps
some racial memory held them there—
an isolate people, a name carried far
only in the wind's harsh sibilance,
its branch-lashing rattle and rush.

Rhiannon

Bones scattered around her bed
like feast-spill, hands gloved with blood
of the newborn she had killed—
so midwives swore, were believed,

thus her punishment to tell
what she had denied to all,
and soon a lie the law bound
her speak had become more real

than heart truth too long buried,
would sit unknowing beside
the flaxen-haired child until
she was told it was her blood

that pulsed his veins, and she called
in the bards so songs could fill
the great hall like uncaged birds,
all in praise of Rhiannon.

Dylan Thomas

Scawmy, gray-souled November
blinds the whale-road, pall draper
over this ship bearing one
whose name means *of the ocean*
in a language he denied
allegiance to, though his lines
rang with cynghanedd—English
reined in by Celtic music,
stitched tight as the coracle
that wombed Taliesin—tribal
rain-downs of sound, not enough:
a small people lose their tongue
one poet at a time. Talent-
squanderer, fraud, miscreant,
apt sobriquets for a life
lived badly between the lines.
The coast recedes. Last gulls cry.
Down in the hold his drunk wife
smokes and flirts with the seamen
who play cards on his coffin.

The Code

The code said any man who asked received
more than food and shelter, safety too,
so when a stranger came out of the night
with bloodstains on his shirt, MacGregor knew
what his obligations were and shared
his hearth and meat and whiskey. Soon enough
a pack of hounds leaped baying at the door,
with them men who wore MacGregor tartan,
kin seeking one who killed one of their own.
The old man turned them back into the dark,
then led his guest across the hills to where
a boat could be procured. Upon that shore
one favor would be asked, a favor granted.
MacGregor dipped the shirt into the loch,
washed his only son's blood from the cloth.

When Serpents Came

Whiterock Mountain: 1912

Five years after in Europe,
two brothers would remember
that November satinbacks
flowed down the face of Whiterock
like hellish tears, close behind
lashes of flame that drove them
from winter rock-lairs toward men
digging firebreaks, and to save
their farms and families men stayed
when smoke muffled sight, ditch floors
came sudden alive with sounds
like a stirred-up beehive, snakes
heard before seen, the rest felt
twined around boot or calf, struck
with shovels, the cold flesh cleaved
as that wide grave grew wider
until the fire was turned back,
and when the smoke cleared the men rose
from trenches where snakes died slow,
twitching like severed limbs.

Shiloh: 1801

God-slain, the multitudes lay
scattered and heaped, campsite washed
in the blood, prayers shouted
over groans and cries before
the fallen rose, their old lives
no more than waning shadow,
as if ghosts of the unborn.

Cold Harbor

Before the hell-storm of lead
left five acres coated blue
and the field writhed and wailed
and mudholes pooled with blood,
before Lee faced Grants' numbers
in eight minutes flat and the sun
gave history three more syllables
and the armies packed up and moved on
to find another place to murder,
before yellow jacket and buzzard,
bluebottle and photographer
came and went about their business,
men sit by campfires and print
their addresses, God-given names
on sheets of paper to pin
on the backs of their uniforms,
and one man raises his pencil
to the middle of a diary
and writes his final entry:
June 3, Cold Harbor. I was killed.

The Crossing

Fog never lifts, though the days
pass as he makes his way home
from Shiloh, the peach orchard
where, left for dead, he awoke

shrouded in petals, the war
a far thunder—deserted
not deserting, home leave bought
by a blue coat stained deep red.

He crosses the boundary line
into Carolina, and soon
mountains pause, let land quick-fall
as light like a dawn breaks through,

reveals his cabin below,
his wife washing clothes, seen for
the first time in months, but when
he comes to Flynn Creek a door

shuts before him, the valley
slowly recedes, and he knows
what he is, knows he must leave
all of what's beloved, alone

but dips his hand in water
for a moment first, watches
it shape-shift like melted ice,
as his kneeling wife pauses,

wrists in flow, feels a known hand
brush her hand, looks up to see
his shade walking the ridge path
leading back to Tennessee.

The Pact

Fog thick as cotton this dawn
five cousins sharing one name
meet at the mouth of Dismal,
Christmas gifts of brass-capped shells
bulging their pockets, bright knives
hip-worn like wallets, for one
a first shotgun the others
pass hand to hand, each truing
the sights with their clan's gray eyes
before given back and they
follow Laurel Fork deeper
into the gorge, boys who
share drinks from the same dipper
baling hay in July, share plugs
of tobacco as they top
rows of burley, but no chores
this late December morning,
free to hunt all day, but they
return at noon, the youngest
carried in their arms, his leg
a red explosion of bone,
the others wounded too, palms
slashed across lifelines, shared blood
shared again, blood-oath made so
no one of them alone will
bear pity or blame, carried
the same way they will carry
the coffin, to the grave.

Abandoned Still on Dismal Mountain

At first a truck radiator sprouting
improbably in this laurel slick—
too far a haul to get rid of,
to hide if theft. I stumble
on coiled copper, know what it is,
or was, the radiator rusty,
the logs mushroomed, mossy,
a wind and rain tumble
of tubing and quart mason jars.
Perhaps he left for greener pastures
of marijuana, or his stingy fire
smoke signaled the sheriff or simply
grew too old to make this climb
and go back burdened to lighten the mind,
the burlap sack clinking and clanking.

The Belt

The uniform he had worn
in the Confederate War
was soon work-worn to a few
dark-blue quilt scraps, sword and hat
bartered in town for coffee
and salt, the belt alone saved
because its buckle saved him
deflecting a sniper's shot,
so kept close at hand always,
while he worked his fields, weekends
its brass eagle buffed for church,
knowing the need for good luck
comes more than once in a life,
so worn the night hard rain made
Running Bear Prong a river
the cabin breaking apart
nail by square nail, the newborn
in his arms when beams buckled,
spilling daughter and father
out of the cabin, and both
believed drowned until dawn when
they found the child, safe and dry
in a white oak, on her chest
the eagle, its talons taut
so it might hold one child aloft.

Good Friday, 2006: Shelton Laurel

Below this knoll a man kneels.
Face close to the earth, he works
soil like a potter works clay,
kneading and shaping until
hands slowly open, reveal
a single green stalk before
he palms himself up the row
as if he hauls on his back
morning's sun-sprawl, a bringer
of light he cannot bring here
where oak trees knit tight shadows
across the marble that marks
the grave of David Shelton.
Thirteen years old, he had asked
one mercy, not to be shot
like his father—in the face.
He shares this grave with the others
hauled back in the snow that night
by kin so their bodies could
darken Shelton ground. Wind lifts
the leaves, grows still. A man sows
his field the old way. The land
unscrolls like a palimpsest.

V

Reading the Leaves

Across the creek, vines of fog
twine around poplar and oak,
distance dimming white, the world
grown close and older, and here
my uncle's workboots dirt-clogged
and dew-dark as he follows
the long sentence of each row,
pauses to thumb through damp leaves,
check close for blue mold, cutworm,
moving slow across a plot
of bottomland whose ending
is a barn, its tin roof spread
like a facedown book to hold
gold leaves of tobacco bound
to rafters, brittle pages
layered by time and weather,
strung together as Celts once
strung leaves on cords to compose
the first words of Albion.

Waterdogs

You can live a life without
knowing they exist if sky
is something glanced out windows,
clouds are spread out scrolls written
in a lost tongue. To find such
small, ephemeral rainbows
what is above must matter,
must be looked for in August
from a wide field where cornstalks
pant and stagger, tobacco
threatens to cure months early.
You must be a man who scuffs
his boot toe against loose skiffs
of dust, searching to find dirt,
then looks up, passing clouds read
like pages turned in a book
to find these damasked commas
which promise coming thunder.

Satinback

Lethal head cut off, it still
outstretched a yardstick when draped
on the barn's broad back, and each
scale peeled off had the rough feel
of a callus, yet soft when
finger traced from neck to where
seven buttons blunted its end,
the black skin so black it hued
into the deepest purple,
the word alive to the touch,
as two smooth syllables slid
off my tongue, before the last
struck against the air like fangs.

Boy in a Boxcar

Smell of creosote, two rails,
knit by crossties, stitched across
the riverbank's brow, I sit
in the boxcar's wide, squared mouth,
legs dangling off, palms pressed flat,
watch from trapped dark the sun wake
grass-stars harbored in dew beads,
ignite a burnished flame on
the French Broad as water makes
a deeper track through Asheville,
hauls its cargo of bottles,
stray planks and stick clots, all else
last night's thunder shook from banks.
Wheels underneath me break free
from years of rust, creak and turn,
westbound, Madison County's
higher mountains—the river
slowing, then still.

Pentecost

Shingles flapped and scattered off
the roof like frightened chickens,
rain didn't fall but slanted,
bruised stained glass to a purple
too dark for scripture, just hymns
sung from memory, sung soft
like whispers as I listened
to wind gusts sucking at nails,
planks shuddering, the steeple
creaking like a ship's masthead,
so closed my eyes, imagined
marble stones cast like anchors
behind the church over years
to hold those crossbeams upright
on that high wave of mountain.

Watauga County: 1962

Smell of honeysuckle bright
as dew beads stringing lines on
the writing spider's silk page,
night's cool lingering, the sun
awake but still lying down,
its slant-light seeping through gaps
of oak branches as the first
blackberry pings the milk pail's
emptiness, begins the slow
filling up, the plush feel of
berry only yesterday
a red-green knot before steeped
in dark to deepest purple,
and as dawn passes, the pail
grows heavy, wearies my arm
until I sit down inside
that maze of briar I make
my kingdom, lift to my mouth
the sweet wine of blackberry
my hands stained like royalty.

Offering

Wear this, my grandmother said,
lifting a shirt from the drawer,
well worn though unworn three months,
one button missing, elbows
threadbare though cover enough
against the dew-cold and chaff
of hay and twine as I stacked
bale after bale in the loft,
breathing the sweetness of fields
mingled with sweat when tin held
splashes of sun like a pan
in that high hall of a room
built by the man whose cloth spilled
over my wrists like a robe,
what he had sown offered up
from his sons' hands to my own.

Water Quilt

The truck bed blossomed with sleep's cloth
each April my grandmother made
her son cross the parkway, jolt down
old logging roads to Laurel Creek,
the only water she believed
pure enough to rinse away the silt
of work grime, worry, fever,
mother and son unfurling
what she had stitched together,
working each quilt like a seine
through current quickened to white,
soaked so thoroughly some part
of water stayed in the cloth,
flowed through it forever,
so she told me one night,
let my fingers confirm
the bed's cool, damp surface
before my eyes closed and I slept
deep beneath the whisper of water.

Raspberries

Dangling in dew-light they were
ruby thimbles set among
an inverted pincushion
of brambles, and like rubies
bright was not best. Dark hues stored
more of that sweetness, just as
their flavor seemed deepest not
when picked but on later dawns
when frost clouded window panes
like paraffin, and what filled
jars lifted from the gloaming
of springhouse shelves spread a warm
slow savor over the tongue.

The Barn-Fox

Each night I believed it leaped
off the barn, out of its death,
loped through the pasture into
the woods, and though in my bed,
I followed—across the creek,
under barbed wire to where trees
pinched star-wicks, made dark darker
as we ranged deeper, hoarfrost
a thin crunching underfoot,
the wind we raised our nose to
rich with prey-scent, and as dawn
pinked ridges and peaks, our prints
receding in the dew.

In a Deerstand Above Goshen Creek

Like a raft snagged in trees after flood,
the deerstand swayed and creaked, moored by
my faith in rusty nails, gray planks,
and when no high-branched buck, spiked yearling
came that afternoon I turned my back
to earth, closed my eyes and did not wake
until darkness settled like rain, stars
emerged like mayflies to depth the night
as I dreamed between earth and sky,
of falling away from earth, toward heaven.

Price Lake

The bluegills, browns, and rainbows
dangled from shiny metal
my father had thrown like chain
in the shallows. The noon sun
shivered the water's surface
like mirage while snake doctors
darned the air with their purple
and green needles. My bobber
snagged again in the cattails,
I entered a grabble of briars,
tightroped the creekboard to where
my parents lay on a bank
softened by cove-moss, each turned
to the other, my mother's
hand tucked inside my father's
half-buttoned shirt, his fingers
brushing ground-lint from her hair,
and in that moment I knew
I did not belong to them,
not in that moment, so slipped
away unnoticed, and though
the gift of that summer took
years to unveil, something stirred
even that day when they came
back to me, my mother's waist
cradled by my father's arm,
his free hand reaching to lift
the stringer. I remember
how it surfaced glistening
like a crystal chandelier,
the fish shimmering color
as if raised in prism-light.

ACKNOWLEDGMENTS

Appalachian Heritage: "Offering," "Raspberries"
Appalachian Journal: "Watauga County, 1962"
Bat City Review: "The Barn-Fox"
Chattahoochee Review: "Cold Harbor
Carolina Quarterly: "Junk Car in Snow," "Watauga County, 1959"
Cortland Review: "Price Lake"
Doubletake: "The Wallet," "Tobacco"
Five Points: "In a Deerstand at Night"
Gin Bender Review: "The Pact"
Hudson Review: "Three A.M. and the Stars Were Out"
Iron Mountain Review: "Pentecost"
Nantahala Review: "Watauga County, 1962"
North Carolina Literary Review: "Genealogy," "Rebecca Boone"
Oxford American: "Pocketknives"
Passages North: "Rhiannon," "Muskellunge," "Blue Cat"
Ploughshares: "Dylan Thomas," "Good Friday, 2006: Shelton
    Laurel."
Quadrant (Australia): "The Trout in the Springhouse,"
    "In a Dry Country," "When Serpents Came," "Milking
    Traces"
Sewanee Review: "Emrys," "The Reaping," "Boy in a Boxcar"
Shenandoah: "Bloodroot," "The Crossing," "White Wings,"
    "Elegy for Merle Watson"
Southern Poetry Review: "Hearth," "Sleepwalking," "Woman
    Among Lightning"
Southern Review: "Charley Starnes," "Shadetree," "Mirror,"
    "Reading the Leaves," "Waterdogs"
Texas Review: "Tobacco Barn"
Wind: "First Memory"

HUB CITY
PRESS

HUB CITY PRESS is an independent press in Spartanburg, South Carolina, that publishes well-crafted, high-quality works by new and established authors, with an emphasis on the Southern experience. We are committed to high-caliber novels, short stories, poetry, plays, memoir, and works emphasizing regional culture and history. We are particularly interested in books with a strong sense of place.

Hub City Press is an imprint of the non-profit Hub City Writers Project, founded in 1995 to foster a sense of community through the literary arts. Our metaphor of organization purposely looks backward to the nineteenth century when Spartanburg was known as the "hub city," a place where railroads converged and departed.

Hub City Press *poetry*

Eureka Mill • Ron Rash

Noticing Eden • Majory Wentworth

Twenty • Kwame Dawes, editor

Still Home • Rachel Harkai, editor

Checking Out • Tim Peeler

Home Is Where • Kwame Dawes, editor